Hippos

Patricia Kendell

HODDER
Wayland

An imprint of Hodder Children's Books

Alligators Chimpanzees Dolphins Elephants
Giraffes Gorillas Grizzly Bears Hippos
Leopards Lions Orangutans Pandas Penguins
Polar Bears Rhinos Sea Otters Sharks Tigers

© 2003 White-Thomson Publishing Ltd

Produced for Hodder Wayland by White-Thomson Publishing Ltd

Editor: Kay Barnham
Designer: Tim Mayer
Consultant: Karen Paolillo – founder of the Turgwe Hippo Trust
Language Consultant: Norah Granger – Senior Lecturer in Primary
    Education at the University of Brighton
Picture research: Shelley Noronha – Glass Onion Pictures

Published in Great Britain in 2003 by Hodder Wayland,
an imprint of Hodder Children's Books.

The right of Patricia Kendell to be identified as the author of this
Work has been asserted by her in accordance with the Copyright,
Designs and Patents Act 1988.

All instructions, information and advice given in this book are
believed to be reliable and accurate. All guidelines and warnings
should be read carefully and the author, packager, editor and publisher cannot accept responsibility for injuries or damage arising out
of failure to comply with the same.

Photograph acknowledgements:
Bruce Coleman 1 & 7 (Carol Hughes), 17 (HPH Photography),
6, 15 & 32 (Jorg & Petra Wegner); FLPA 5 (Gerard Lacz),
14 (Albert Visage), 28 (Terry Whittaker); Images of Africa
Photobank 29 (David Keith Jones); K Paolillo 8, 21, 23;
OSF 4 (Rafi Ben-Shahar), 16 (Richard Packwood),
25 (Edward Parker), 19, 22 (Alan Root), 20 (Leonard Lee Rue),
12 (Steve Turner); Still Pictures 10, 18 (M & C Denis-Huot),
27 (Mark Edwards), 13, 26 (Mathieu Laboureur), 9 (Yves Lefevre),
24 (Fritz Polking).

British Library Cataloguing in Publication Data
Kendell, Patricia
    Hippopotamus. – (In the wild)
    1. Hippopotamus – Juvenile literature
    I. Title II. Barnham, Kay
    599.6'35

ISBN: 0 7502 4229 9

Printed and bound in Hong Kong

Hodder Children's Books
A division of Hodder Headline Limited
338 Euston Road, London NW1 3BH

Produced in association with WWF-UK.
WWF-UK registered charity number 1081247.
A company limited by guarantee number 4016725.
Panda device © 1986 WWF ® WWF registered trademark owner.

The website addresses (URLs) included in this book were valid at
the time of going to press. However, because of the nature of the
Internet, it is possible that some addresses may have changed, or
sites may have changed or closed down since publication. While
the author, packager and publisher regret any inconvenience this
may cause readers, no responsibility for any such changes can be
accepted by either the author, packager or the publisher.

Contents

Where hippos live

The great African hippopotamus lives in rivers near grassland in Africa.

The much smaller pygmy hippopotamus
lives in the **rainforests** of western Africa.
A hippopotamus is known as a hippo.

Baby hippos

A baby hippo is born at the edge of a river among the **reeds**. It is called a calf. It can swim and walk very soon after it is born.

The calf will drink milk from its mother
for about 18 months.

Looking after the calves

Mother hippos protect their calves from dangerous enemies such as crocodiles.

Mother and baby stay close together.
This calf is climbing on to its mother's back,
where it is comfortable and safe.

Family life

One older male, a group of females and their young live together in a **herd**. Young males live together in separate groups. Mother hippos look after each other's babies.

Guarding the herd

The chief male in a herd will fight any younger male who dares to enter his **territory**.

These fights are very fierce. In the end,
a very old male will have to let a younger,
stronger male take over the herd.

A watery world

Hippos spend up to 14 hours a day in the water.
They can stay underwater for as long as five minutes,
closing their **nostrils** to keep the water out.

Their eyes, ears and nose are on the top of their head so that they can lie low in the water and still see and hear.

Keeping cool

Hippos need to stay in the water to keep cool in the hot sun. A special, pink fluid oozes from their skin. This protects them from sunburn.

If the river dries up, hippos will **wallow**
in mud to keep cool.

Hippo friends

Hippos will happily let birds sit on their backs. The birds catch the irritating flies that buzz around.

Under the water, hippos let fish nibble away
at the tiny plants that grow on their skin.

Eating

Towards evening, hippos leave the water and follow well-known paths in search of grass and other plants.

Hippos use their huge lips to cut the grass.
The places where they have eaten the grass
are known as 'hippo lawns'.

On the move

The huge African hippo moves gracefully underwater, by walking on the bottom of the river or lake.

Hippos can be **aggressive**, and will **charge** if they feel threatened.

Threats...

People kill hippos for meat. They sell their ivory teeth, and use hippo skin to make **cattle whips**.

Farmers plant crops where hippos live.
Then they shoot the hippos when they
eat these crops.

...and dangers

All hippos are in danger because the places where they live are being destroyed or taken over by people.

The pygmy hippo is in the greatest danger
because much of its forest home has
already been cut down.

Helping hippos to survive

The shy pygmy hippo will only survive in the future if its forest home is protected.

Tourists enjoy coming to see the great African hippos
in **national parks**. Here people can learn more about
what hippos need to survive in the future.

Further information

Find out more about how we can help hippos in the future.

ORGANIZATIONS TO CONTACT

WWF-UK
Panda House, Weyside Park,
Godalming, Surrey GU7 1XR
Tel: 01483 426444
http://www.wwf.org.uk

Care for the Wild International
1 Ashfolds, Horsham Road, Rusper,
West Sussex RH12 4QX
Tel: 01293 871596
http://www.careforthewild.org.uk

Turgwe Hippo Trust
Hippo Haven
PO Box 322
Chiredzi
Zimbabwe
Tel: 00 263 24 456
http://www.savethehippos.com

BOOKS

Hippos (The Giant Animals series):
Marianne Johnston, Rosen Publishing
Group 1999.

The Hippopotamus (Animal Close-Ups):
Christine Denis-Huot, Charlesbridge
Publishing 1994.

For more able readers:

Hippos (Zoobooks Series): Beth Wagner
Brust, Wildlife Education Ltd 2001.

Hippos (Naturebooks): Jenny Markert,
Child's World Inc. 2001.

Glossary

WEBSITES

Most young children will need adult help when visiting websites. Those listed have child-friendly pages to bookmark.

http://www.thebigzoo.com
This site has information for more fluent readers and video sequences of hippos in zoos such as getting out of the water, feeding and yawning.

http://www.hippos.com
This site has video sequences of hippos and information about how to help them survive.

aggressive – ready to attack.

cattle whips – whips used to guide cattle and keep them together.

charge – run very quickly towards someone or something.

herd – a group of animals that stay together.

national parks – protected areas where animals can live safely.

nostrils – the openings on an animal's nose that let in the air.

rainforests – forests in hot, wet places.

reeds – plants with tall, strong stems that grow in and near water.

territory – the home area of an animal.

wallow – to roll in the mud.

Index